The Birth of a SAVIOR

Adapted by Tess Fries

Illustrated by Cheryl Mendenhall

Art Direction by
Shannon Osborne Thompson

All art and editorial material is owned by Dalmatian Press.
ISBN: 1-57759-512-2

The DALMATIAN PRESS name, logo and spotted design are
trademarks of Dalmatian Press, Franklin, Tennessee 37067.

11450a/The Birth of a Savior

The Roman ruler, Caesar Augustus, had commanded everyone to travel to the town where their family was from, in order to be counted. Men, women, and children of all ages went on their journey by donkeys or shuffled slowly along the road.

Mary and Joseph were traveling, too. Joseph's family was from Bethlehem. He and Mary had to travel the long way there — even though Mary was going to have a baby very soon. No one could disobey the ruler's command.

Many months
before this
journey, the
angel, Gabriel,
had appeared to
Mary with a
special message
from God.

Gabriel told Mary that through the Holy Spirit she would have a son and that his name would be "Jesus." The angel said, "Jesus will be great, and his kingdom will last forever. He will be called the 'Son of God.'"

Now, as they traveled, Mary knew that it would soon be time for this remarkable baby to be born.

At last they arrived in Bethlehem. How good it would feel to stop and get a cool drink of water! Joseph went from inn to inn looking for one that had a room where he and Mary could rest, but every inn was full with the many travelers that had come to Bethlehem. Finally Joseph led Mary to a stable where she could lie down.

That night, in the dark and damp of the stable, the baby Jesus was born. Mary tenderly wrapped him in soft swaddling clothes and laid him in the manger.

Not far from the stable, shepherds were in a field watching their sheep during the night.

Suddenly an angel of the Lord came to them and a bright light shone all around them. The shepherds were afraid!

But the angel said, "Fear not, for I bring you tidings of great joy which shall be to all people. For unto you is born this day in the city of David, a Savior, which is Christ the Lord. And you shall find the baby wrapped in swaddling clothes and lying in a manger."

All at once there were many angels singing, praising God and saying, "Glory to God in the highest — may there be peace on earth, and good will toward men."

W hen the
beautiful singing
was over and
the angels went
back to heaven,
the shepherds
said to one
another, "Let us
go to Bethlehem
and see the child
God has told
us about!"

The shepherds left their flocks of sheep and hurried to the city. There, in the humble stable, they found Mary and Joseph. The baby Jesus was lying on straw in the manger.

How excited they were! They left the stable full of joy and told everyone the message the angel had delivered to them.

As they walked back to the fields, they praised God for the things they had seen and heard.

The Savior had come — born in a simple stable.

Through His teachings and His sacrifice, He would give us eternal life — the greatest gift of all.

"and she gave birth to her firstborn, a son.
She wrapped him in cloths and placed him in a manger,
because there was no room for them in the inn."
Luke 2:7
(NIV)